THE METEORA

MONASTERY VISITING HOURS

BARLAAM

9-1 and 3.30-6 daily
except Fridays

METAMORPHOSIS
(GREAT METEORON)

9-1 and 3-6 daily
except Tuesdays

SAINT STEPHEN'S

8-12 and 3-6 daily
except Mondays

SAINT NICHOLAS
ANAPAFSAS

9-1 and 3-6 daily

ROUSANOU

9-1 and 3-6 daily

AGHIA TRIADA

9-6 daily

THE VIRGIN
YPAPANTI

Closed

Greek National Tourist Organisation
(E.O.T./G.N.T.O.) of Kalambaka
5 28th October Street, Kalambaka
Tel. (0432) 24444

N

✝ Varlaám Ⓟ ☎

aos
s

Roussánou ☎ Ⓟ

viacnava

Aghía Triás

Ⓟ ✝ ☎ Aghios Stéfanos

K A L A B A K A

CAMPING:
Kalambaka

Ⓟ ☎

🚌

TRIKALA — LARISSA — VOLOS →

CAMPING:
International

Edition: Georg. Tziqras-Kalabaka

CONTENTS

THE METEORA
A BRIEF HISTORY

The Meteora, drawn by B. Barskij. 1745

Conspicuous in more than one sense, the monastic settlements of the Meteora perch upon huge and precipitous rocks that rise abruptly from the north-western edge of the Thessalian plain where it meets the foothills of the massive Pindos mountain range. The strangely varied landscape that has few parallels anywhere in the world strikes the traveller with a curious mixture of awe and amazement.

Men contemptuous of the world became hermits on these weird vast rocks and here they found spiritual tranquility in prayer and endured the extreme deprivations of the anchorite

The Rock of the Holy Spirit

Confronted by this magnificent scene, wild and imposing in wintertime when the north winds howl through the confusion of rock masses but subdued and docile in sun-drenched days laden with the mountain scents of the wild flowers and shrubs bordering the defiles separating the rocks, the visitor senses the insignificance of human existence in infinity and enters upon his pilgrimage. Enveloped by nature in a wilderness that offers only solitude with but one consolation, the swift flight of birds and the muffled sound of the semandron in a nearby monastery, he finds himself close to his creator.

For centuries now an otherworldly calm has pervaded the towering grey rocks that provide eagles' eeries high above the encroaching plain, while great monasteries, humble chapels and now long-deserted hermitages cling to their pinnacles.

The monastic community that came into being in this impressive rocky landscape is unique in the world, while the astonishing natural phenomenon that gave it its existence is of great geological age and has long been the subject of study by many Greek and foreign geologists and scientists. Its most probable origin is the one suggested by the German Al. Philippson in his work on Thessaly and Epiros (1897). He holds that this complex of colossal rocks emerged from the delta region of a great river which flowed for thousands of years into the narrow but deep sector of the sea that then covered the whole of what is today the plain of Thessaly.

It was here that many anchorites chose to settle, on the summits of the soaring rocks half way between earth and sky, seeking to live close to God for the remainder of their years while turning their backs upon mundane things and devoting themselves to prayer and spiritual contemplation.

According to tradition, the first hermits to seek solitude among these immense outcrops of rock settled on the Meteora long before the 10th century of our era. They lived in caves and crevices in the rock face and contrived small oratories where they dedicated themselves to prayer and to constant study of early Orthodox texts.

Their religious duties, however, required them to attend the Liturgy and to receive the Holy Eucharist and these rites called for the presence of a priest. At first they were obliged to attend divine service in the old church of the Archangels and later, once it had been built, in the church of the Theotokos. Eventually the First Skete (Proti Skiti) of Doupiani was founded; it was placed under the jurisdiction of the bishopric of Stagi.

The founding of the Skete of Doupiani some time in the 11th century marked the beginning of coenobitic life and of an organized monastic community on the Meteora. Common attendance at the Liturgy on Sundays and the partaking together of the Holy Eucharist were to lead those early ascetics into forming a spiritual brotherhood, and in the course of time to the establishment first of the Monastery of Doupiani and then of the church of the Protaton after the manner of the church of the same name on Mount Athos. The abbot was appointed Protos or superior; he resided in the monastery and exercised religious authority over the whole community.

Two or three centuries were to pass in tranquility, but the 13th and 14th centuries were disturbed by incursions of Franks, Serbs, Catalans, Albanians, and Turks, each aspiring to conquer the territory of Thessaly. During the reign of the Byzantine emperor Andronikos the Younger (1328-1344) the king of Serbia, Stefan Dušan, was declared king of the Serbians, Romaioi, Albanians, and Bulgars and occupied Thessaly and neighbouring provinces. He appointed Grigorios Preliub as local governor and his half-brother Symeon as despot of Aetolia.

The monk Athanasios, hounded from Mount Athos by corsairs' raids, reached the Meteora in 1334 accompanied by his confessor Father Grigorios; they settled on the Stylo ton Stagon (Stagi Column), remaining there for ten years.

St. Anthony's hermitage

*Destitute hermits who have turned their backs upon the world live in caves on
these precipitous rocks with a chasm below and the calls of eagles above.
Here they pray night and day, beseeching God grant their souls eternal rest.
Countless such men have breathed their last here, in isolation and oblivion.*

Athanasios the Meteorite, later Blessed Athanasios, had but one purpose in mind, to establish a monastery regulated in the same orderly manner as the religious houses on Athos. In 1344 he gathered around him fourteen monks from the neighbourhood and scaled Platys Lithos (literally, Broad Stone), a huge rock rising to 613 metres above the sea and to 413 metres above the town of Kalambaka. There he and his companions commenced what was for those times the truly titanic task of erecting the earliest of the buildings that later became the famous monastery of the Great Meteoron. It was this pious monk who laid down the rules governing the conduct of coenobitic life on the Meteora.

Following the deaths of Stefan Dušan and of Prelium, Symeon declared himself king and tzar and united Thessaly and Epiros, making Trikala their capital city.

Symeon was a very devout man and greatly assisted the monasteries of the Meteora with gifts of money and the grant of special privileges in 1358 and 1363. By his decree the monastery of Doupiani acquired complete independence, thenceforth being no longer subject to the see of Stagi, but to the jurisdiction of the Protos of the skete, at that time the monk Neilos.

A God-fearing ruler, Symeon died in 1371 leaving his son Ioannis Uroš Palaiologos, then studying on Mount Athos, to succeed him. On his return to Thessaly to assume his throne Ioannis went up to the Meteora and there met Athanasios. The young ruler was deeply moved, not only by the serenity of monastic life and the personal qualities of Athanasios, but also by the shunning of the world of the flesh by monks who envisioned an everlasting world of the spirit in heaven. His attachment to Athanasios was with bonds of true friendship and affection and of profound respect for the task which Athanasios was accomplishing with such prudence and patience in a spirit of Christian dedication. He abdicated his throne and, choosing the difficult path of a humble monk,

became Brother Ioasaph.

After eleven years of unclouded collaboration with Ioasaph, resulting in the monastery's continuous growth and increasing influence, Athanasios died and was buried in his monastery. Ioasaph succeeded him as abbot and completed the task he and Athanasios had jointly begun. While pious folk were endowing the monastery with gifts of land and property they renovated the church of the Metamorphosis, built by Athanasios, and added a number of new cells and an infirmary for the monks. Ioasaph showed both wisdom and ability in exercising his rule over the monastic community. He was succeeded in turn by Symeon, an Epirot, who likewise achieved renown in carrying on the work that was pleasing in the sight of God.

The grandeur of the landscape and the security from raiders, robbers, and malefactors enjoyed by the monks living on the barely accessible summits of those precipitous rocks led over the years to the creation of a large, closely knit community comprising many monasteries supported by numerous donations and privileges granted by devout rulers and noblemen. The consequence was that many clerics, not all of them known to us by name, became founders of monasteries including those of Aghia Triada, Saint Stephen, Ypapantis, Rousanou or Arsanou, Saint George Mandilas, Saint Nicholas Anapafsas, the Virgin of Mykani, Saints Theodore, Saint Nicholas Bandova-Kophina, The Holy Apostles, Saint Grigorios, Saint Antony Pantokratoros, Prodromou, Aghia Moni, Ypsiloteras Kalligraphon, Modestos, Proskyniseos, Alysos, Apostle Peter, Saint Dimitrios, Kallistratou, and the Archangels.

Later there set in a gradual decline in this theocratic community. Today only six monasteries are still functioning: Metamorphosis, Barlaam, Saint Nicholas Anapafsas, Rousanou, Aghia Triada, and Saint Stephen's. As for the rest, some have fallen into ruin while of others all trace has vanished.

Cresting these great rocky eminences, the monasteries of the Metamorphosis and of Barlaam seem poised between earth and sky in their endeavour to reach closer to God in heaven.

13

KALAMBAKA

Kalambaka lies at the western edge of the Thessalian plain, where the great peaks of the Pindos range have their origin, and at the foot of the vast rocks of the Meteora.

The historians Strabo and Livy referred to the city in antiquity as Aiyinion. Destroyed by Roman conquerors in 167 B.C., its remaining inhabitants managed to rebuild it and the town survived for several centuries, until about the 11th century of our era. Mentioned in historical documents of that time by the name of Stagi, it was the see of the bishopric of the same name.

Later, during the years of Ottoman rule, the inhabitants called it Kalambaka though the bishopric retained its name even when it was merged in 1899 with the see of Trikala, still known today as the see of Trikki and Stagi.

The Swedish traveller J.J. Björnstaal visited the town in 1779 and has left us a description of old Kalambaka:

"After three hours on horseback we reached the Greek village of Stagoi which the Turks call Kalambak and where there are ten Christian churches but no mosque... Visit to the seat of the Metropolitan to which one ascends only by dint of great effort, for the Christians of the place have to build dwellings of such difficulty of access in order to enjoy security. The Metropolitan is absent. Because of the Albanians, he has taken refuge in a more secure place, in the monastery of Saint Stephen.

"As the village lies exactly below the most precipitous high rocks, climbing from one rock pile to the next involves one in great exertion and danger. The rocks are vertical and astonishingly high. Some are nothing less than round stone blocks, heaped one on top of another as in a column..."

Nikolaos Magnis who also visited Kalambaka, a few years prior to 1860, wrote:

"Stagoi, formerly known as Gomphoi and now as Kalambaka. A Christian hamlet with about 250 dwellings, three hours distant from Trikala, and the see of a bishop within the jurisdiction of the Metropolitan of Larisa. Close to the frontiers of Epiros in the foothills of the Pindos range, on the left bank of the Pineios river."

Kalambaka possesses one very notable monument: the Cathedral Church of the bishopric of Stagi. It was built in the 10th or 11th century over the ruins of an early Christian church. Dedicated to the Dormition of the Virgin, it is a three-aisled basilica without a dome.

Outstanding among the church's treasures is the marble pulpit, unique in all Greece. As it stands precisely in the centre, in front of the Royal Doors of the Sanctuary, its imposing form dominates the scene in a most striking manner. The spiritual leader of the congregation mounts the high pulpit to preach the word of God by steps ranged on either side of it.

Wonderful wall-paintings that date to the 12th century and some others executed in 1573 by the priest Kyriazis and Neophytos, son of the great Cretan painter Theophanis, decorate the church's interior. They are in an excellent state of preservation, as is also the remarkable carved wooden ikonostasis.

The chrysobull issued by Emperor Andronikos in 1330 confirming the privileges of the bishopric of Stagi and also the sigillum signed by Antonios Patriarch of Constantinople in 1393 are reproduced in the narthex.

Kalambaka with (left) the monastery of Aghia Triada and (right) the monastery of Saint Peter on Alysos

View of Kalambaka

A marble ciborium overhangs the altar in the sanctuary; at the back of the altar is the throne in which the prelate used to sit and rest. Beneath the throne is a large crypt in which Christians once took refuge from infidel raiders and malefactors.

Nowadays Kalambaka offers visitors coming to visit the Meteora, barely five kilometers away, good accommodation in hotels with all modern facilities. The town lies at a distance of 21 kilometres from Trikala, 83 from Larisa, 105 from Ioannina, 140 from Volos, 285 from Thessaloniki, and 326 from Athens. The population of the prefecture of Kalambaka, which consists of one municipality, fifty communes, and 81 settlements, numbers about 32,000.

The Byzantine church of the Dormition of the Theotokos (Virgin Mother)

The only solid marble pulpit in Greece stands in the middle of the church of the
Dormition of the Theotokos in Kalambaka

KASTRAKI

This small picturesque village, nestling in the angle of huge rock outcrops that seem to hold it in their protective embrace, lies at the extreme edge of the secular world.

Kastraki is a commune created during the Ottoman occupation out of several smaller settlements by Greeks from Epiros who took refuge here to escape from Ali Pasha, the infamous ruler of Epiros, a Turkish-Albanian whose capital was Ioannina.

A Byzantine fortress, of which few ruins remain, gave its name to the village. In the interwar years the place still retained intact the traditional appearance of a Greek agricultural community. However, with the spread of transportation and the frequent arrival of tourists, it has become a noted holiday centre with camping sites, taverns, and guest houses offering a pleasant stay to visitors to the Meteora.

The sparse vegetation and the rays of the rising sun attempt to tame the wild nature of the huge rocks. The humble pilgrim cannot but respect the awesome character of this landscape.

Kastraki viewed from the air

DOUPIANI

Doupiani

This small church is situated opposite Kastraki on the left-hand side of the road leading up to the monasteries. It is the old kyriakon or main church of the Skete of Stagi. Built early in the 13th century, it was renovated in 1867 and again in 1974.

The church is of rectangular shape and has a tiled timber roof; some wall-paintings have survived, among them two marvellous full-length figures of Christ and the Virgin. A cross inscribed with the letters IC XC NIKA (Jesus Christ Conquers) is carved upon the marble altar stone.

A small church stands in the mouth of a remote cavern on one of the neighbouring outcrops. Consecrated to the memory of Saint George, the church represents a considerable hazard to those who lack experience as climbers. It is known as Saint George Mandilas (the 'Kerchiefer') on account of the variously shaped and coloured kerchiefs, votive offerings of the faithful, that hang upon the grey rock with which their bright hues contrast sharply.

Every year on the saint's feast day the more courageous inhabitants of Kastraki risk their lives in climbing the rock. After lighting a candle before the saint's ikon they offer up a prayer and dedicate a kerchief to the saint who assisted them in their ascent made to honour his memory.

Some vestiges remain of old wooden platforms in this cavern on a gigantic outcrop standing to the right of the way up to the monasteries. Tradition relates that monks who transgressed the severe rules of Orthodox monasticism used to be incarcerated here.

Prison-cells for errant monks

Kastraki

Village houses crouch in fear below the colossal stone pinnacles that rear up threateningly over their roof-tops.

Kastraki

*The monastery of Saint Nicholas Anapafsas
and the Hermitage of the Forerunner,
drawn by B. Barskij, 1745*

THE HOLY MONASTERY OF
SAINT NICHOLAS ANAPAFSAS

Leaving Kastraki and proceeding uphill we enter the stone forest of the Meteora rocks.

The first monastery we meet, to the left of our way, is the monastery of Saint Nicholas Anapafsas perched on the top of a vast rock whose summit is of small surface area. Our admiration is stirred by the architectural form of the buildings, moulded to the shape of the height on which the complex rests.

A short climb and a few steps carved into the rock bring us before the entrance to the monastery. The limited space has determined that its churches and other buildings be constructed at various levels, thus creating a small but labyrinthine cluster.

Entering the lowest floor we discover a tiny chapel dedicated to Saint Antony. The minute sanctuary is barely four square metres in extent, allowing room for only one priest. A small crypt to the left has been converted into a cell.

The church of Saint Nicholas is on the first floor. Decorated with fine wall-paintings, it is long and narrow and of irregular shape with a low windowless dome, the sanctuary unavoidably facing north. The body of the narrow church is illuminated almost exclusively by candle-light. By contrast, the narthex is spacious and well-lit and suggests that it was built to serve as the forecourt of the monastery.

On the second floor is the old refectory, now

used as a reception room, the small church of Saint John the Forerunner, and the ossuary in which many monks' skulls are stored.

The wall-paintings by Theophanis surpass all expectation, confounding even the most demanding aesthete and pricking the conscience of even the greatest of unbelievers. They are the only paintings that bear his signature, those he executed in other monasteries and particularly on Mount Athos being unsigned.

Theophanis Strelitzas or Bathas was born in about 1500 in Crete where he was taught religious painting. Devotion to his religion led him to assume a monk's habit though he was married and the father of two children. His sons were both initiated by their father into hagiography and carried on his work.

All of Theophanis' mural masterpieces are to be found on mainland Greece. In 1527 he decorated the church of Saint Nicholas Anapafsas. Later he went to Mount Athos and painted churches at the monasteries of the Great Lavra and Stavronikita, where he remained for the rest of his days, his highly valued work establishing him as supreme among painters of the Cretan School. Theophanis died in Heraklion, Crete in 1559.

The Cretan School marks the high point of 'Byzantine' painting. Its roots lie not in Crete but in 14th-century Constantinople whence its basic tenets were transmitted to Serbia, Macedonia, Southern Greece, and Mystra; eventually, in the 16th century, it reached Crete where it acquired its final form, the finest examples of which are on Mount Athos.

The church of Saint Nicholas was built at the expense of Dionysios Metropolitan of Larisa and of Nikanor hieromonk and Exarch of Stagi, as recorded in the inscription over the entrance to the church:

THE DIVINE AND ALL-VENERABLE CHURCH OF OUR SAINTED FATHER NIKOLAOS WAS ERECTED FROM ITS FOUNDATIONS BY THE VERY REVEREND METROPOLITAN OF LARISA KYR DIONYSIOS AND THE MOST BLESSED AMONG HIEROMONKS KYR NIKANOR EXARCH OF STAGI AND THE BROTHERS RESIDING THERE. IT WAS DECORATED AT THE EXPENSE OF EVANGELOS KYPRIANOS (1527) THE 12TH DAY OF THE MONTH OF OCTOBER. THE HAND OF THEOPHANIS OF STRELITZA IN CRETE KNOWN ALSO AS BATHAS.

Theophanis displays an incomparable mastery of colour harmony in the facial features of saints which he depicts in light and dark tones according to the joyous or mournful mood he wishes to convey. His brush moves with astonishing ease over the confined and irregular surfaces, leaving no empty spaces and producing a marvellous harmony. It is extremely difficult to single out particular compositions from his entire oeuvre as superior to any others.

The conch in the church sanctuary is decorated with a representation of the Virgin interceding for the faithful; to the left and right of it are the hierarchs Basil and Chrysostom, the Christ of Pity, and figures of other hierarchs. The serene image of Jesus, surrounded by a choir of angels carrying the Sacred Chalice, the Three-branched Lamp, and labara, dominates the dome.

Among other representations are the Prophets, the four Evangelists in the pendentives beneath the dome, and the Dodekaorton (Twelve Feasts), and scenes from the Passion of Christ in the form of small portable ikons.

In the narthex is a depiction of the Second Coming as the painter imagines it, while on the south side are Dionysios and Nikanor, founders of the monastery, praying to the Mother of God and to Saint Athanasios the Meteorite. In addition there is a marvellous wall-painting of the Theotokos with the Christ Child grasping her middle finger, and next to it a rare picture of the Dormition of Saint Nicholas and others of Saint Athanasios and scenes from the miracles of Christ.

e monastery of Saint Nicholas Anapafsas

Late 19th-century engraving of the Holy Monastery of the Theotokos. The monastery is now in ruins, only a few traces of it remaining on the peak of the rock.

The study of old Orthodox texts provides a monk's spiritual fare

Adam names the animals

The church is also adorned with two fine murals of the Dormition of the Blessed Ephraim and of Adam naming the animals; apart from these there are yet others that clearly display Theophanis' exceptional technique.

The attribute Anapafsas may have been the surname of Nikanor, one of the founders of the monastery. But the more accepted explanation is that it arises from the location of the monastery which offers spiritual and physical repose, just as the entire complex of rocks that comprise the Meteora induces that sense of spiritual contentment and ease sought by all men, whether monks or visitors and humble pilgrims to this monastic community.

This utterly beautiful scene scarcely touched by time leaves an indelible impression on all who linger there, if only for a few hours.

Saint Nicholas

The interior of the chur
of Saint Nicholas Anapa

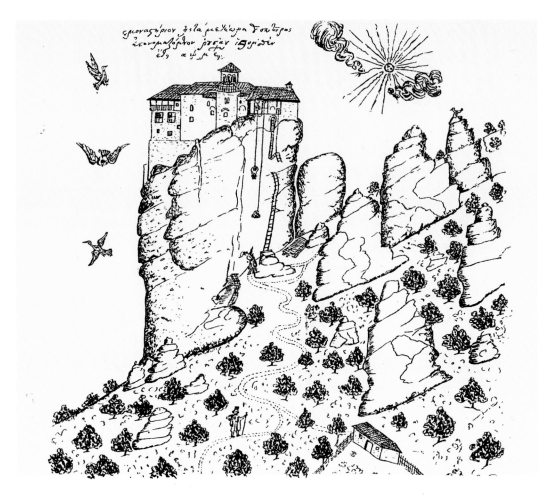

The monastery of Rousanou, drawn by B. Barskij, 1745

THE HOLY MONASTERY OF
R O U S A N O U

The story of this monastery opens with mere tradition, for there is no historical evidence for either a founding date of 1388 or for the origin of the name Rousanou. But the few facts that are known point to a very early date for the foundation of the monastery.

Many people believe that the first settler was called Rousanos who may have come from the village of Rosana. Unverified historical sources suggest that the monastery was founded in 1288 by the hieromonks Nikodimos and Venediktos. What is certain is that in 1545, with the approval of Visarion, Metropolitan of Larisa, and of the abbot of the monastery of the Great Meteoron, the Epirot brothers and hieromonks Ioasaph and Maximos built the katholikon in the Byzantine style over the site of the ruined church of the Metamorphosis of Christ and renovated the monastery which then functioned as a coenobium.

We have no knowledge of the monastery's development in ensuing years. However, a slow decline set in during the two centuries prior to 1940, the place being pillaged from time to time — as were other Meteora monasteries — by invaders of different faiths and by unidentified malefactors. Such treasures and manuscripts as survived these raids are preserved today in the monastery of the Great Meteoron.

For twenty years commencing in 1950 an elderly woman named Efsevia from nearby Kastraki was at pains to keep up this old three-storey building. Following restoration it functions again today as a convent for nuns.

The church of the Metamorphosis and a number of reconstructed cells are on the middle floor, while spacious reception rooms occupy the upper one.

With its sanctuary pointing northwards, the church of the Metamorphosis is a two-columned cruciform building with a dome and narthex. The wall-paintings in the katholikon were executed in 1561, during the abbacy of Arsenios, by artists of the Cretan School but are unsigned; they have been preserved in a very good state, as has also the remarkable carved and gilded wooden ikonostasis.

There are two noteworthy wall-paintings of Saint Barbara on the right. The Pantokrator in the dome has suffered damage from damp. The Resurrection and Transfiguration of Christ are depicted in the choirs; below them are many military saints, while on the south wall are the hymnists Kosmas and Ioannis Damaskinos (John of Damascus) as well as the many-figured scene of the Dormition of the Virgin flanked by the archangels Michael and Gabriel.

The entire narthex is embellished with wall-paintings of exceptional quality. On its west wall are portrayed scenes of the martyrdom of saints, while over the doorway leading into the body of the church there is a Preparation of the Throne — another many-figured scene with angels and mortals and a fiery river. A little higher are three angels, one of whom holds the lists recording the deeds of the soul under judgement and the second the scales of justice, while the third fends off with his trident the devil who is trying to drag away with him to Hell the soul standing trial.

Over the doorway there survives an inscription which reads: THIS ALL-VENERABLE AND HOLY CHURCH OF THE LORD GOD OUR SAVIOUR JESUS CHRIST OF THE META-MORPHOSIS WAS DECORATED WITH THE ASSISTANCE AND THROUGH THE EFFORT AND AT THE EXPENSE OF THE VERY BLESSED AMONG HIEROMONKS KYR AR-SENIOS ABBOT OF THIS VENERABLE MON-ASTERY IN THE YEAR 1561 THE 20TH DAY OF THE MONTH OF NOVEMBER INDICTION 4.

The monastery of Rousanou

The magic of the Meteora landscape:
the monastery of Rousanou viewed from above

In such a place one communes directly with God: the very air is filled with prayer and psalm and with incense whose fragrance permeates the whole monastic settlement.

The monastery of Rousa

The muffled sound of wooden gongs, bird-song, and the sigh of the wind among the towering rocks transport us far from mundane things to the unearthly, ideal worlds of the spirit...

The monastery of Rousanou

39

THE LIFE OF THE MONK

Monasteries are the ornament of Orthodox Christianity. Scattered throughout the length and breadth of Greece, in the mountains, on the plains, in the islands, they continue their age-long history as centres of faith, piety, and tranquility as well as of social service to the community rendered by monks and nuns dedicated to God and to spending their remaining years in prayer, chastity, and poverty.

The first Christian hermits and ascetics to turn their back upon the world appeared at the end of the 3rd century. They devoted themselves to the worship of God and to continual prayer in places remote from everyday society, in caves and destitute sketes.

Many of these men spent the rest of their lives in the solitude of the wilderness they had chosen. Others entered monasteries that had been founded in the meantime and lived with other monks as coenobites, all participating in the Liturgy, joining together in common prayer, and receiving the Holy Eucharist every Sunday.

The Divine Office — the Worship of God — is the chief occupation of monks and nuns in Greek monasteries; inseparable from Orthodox Christianity, it is communion with God, the Holy Eucharist lying at its very core.

The life of a monk revolves around the katholikon, the main church of his monastery. There the Liturgy is celebrated according to the formal canons which are closely observed. This observation of the formal element preserves Orthodox tradition and faithfully perpetuates the institutions of the Church.

Prayer — communion with God — is the foremost task of a monk. He will spend six to seven hours each day — up to eleven hours on Sundays and holy days — at penitence and in devotion, in spiritual contemplation, in the repudiation by the spirit of all that is material, in fasting and in prayer. The worship of God is the monk's prime concern.

Anyone who has attended the Liturgy in a Greek monastery will ever recall the monks chanting and praying in their stalls, the fragrance of incense, the candles illuminating the ascetic figures of saints portrayed in murals and in ikons, and the Pantokrator in the high dome sending down his blessings.

A monastery is ruled by its abbot, a convent by its abbess, each supervising the spiritual welfare of the community. Stavropegic monasteries are directly subject to the Patriarchate of Constantinople, while parochial ones fall under the jurisdiction of the bishop in whose diocese they lie.

A monk involves himself wholeheartedly in his individual occupation whether he is engaged in woodcarving, a handicraft, the painting of portable ikons, farming, or any other pursuit. In former times he might have been a shoemaker, carpenter, gardener, tailor, or miller.

A monk's occupation is not directed towards profit. The income from his labour is donated to philanthropic institutions, maintains schools, or fosters other social causes.

These centres of Orthodoxy fulfilled an important role throughout the period of Ottoman rule· (roughly 1453 to 1828) being instrumental in the continuance of Hellenism, for they supplied the clandestine schools that preserved the Greek's mother tongue; moreover they steadfastly supported Greek irregulars fighting in the war of independence and provided places of refuge for Greeks oppressed and persecuted by the Asiatic power. Because of the help and sustenance they gave, many monasteries were plundered and burnt down and many monks were martyred or murdered.

Christian and Greek tradition, maintained in Greece's religious centres, proved inextinguishable. Orthodox Christianity survived in them and the spiritual heritage of the race was preserved intact.

These monastic communities are today an invaluable element of Greece's cultural inheritance as well as a source of spiritual strength and uplift.

The monastery of Rousanou

The first fogs of autumn mask the tips of these gigantic rocks. Winter is in the offing and during the long ice-bound nights the Meteora landscape becomes ever more imposing and otherworldly.
A strange sensation grips the visitor when the north wind whistles down the defiles that divide the sheer rock faces from each other and the sluggish oil lamps in the monasteries flicker in the tiny windows of monks' cells, sending out their faint message that there is life still in that sombre void.

The late afternoon sun casts its springtime spell over the Meteora scene. Soon it will drop behind the skyline of the Pindos mountains and the immense rocks will throw deeper shadows menacingly across the darkening eastern horizon, filling the bystander with awe and wonderment...

† μαρτυρι
ον τοῦ ἁγι
καὶ ἐνδόξου
μεγαλο μαρ
τυρος τοῦ Χ̅Υ̅
τρύφωνος·
Χ̅ ΕΥ̅Χ̅·

οὑ Κ̅Υ̅ καὶ Θ̅Υ̅ καὶ σ̅ρ̅ σ̅ ἡμ̅
τ̅υ̅ Χ̅Ν̅· μετὰ τὴν θείαν
καὶ θβαμ δρικὴν αὐτοῦ
πρὸς ἁ̅γ̅ιο̅υ̅ θεια̅ δ αμ ζαμ·
καὶ τὴν ἐκ με κρῶν τριὴ
μερον ἔγερσιν· καὶ πρὸς

MONASTIC TREASURES

The sacristies and libraries of the Meteora monasteries comprise one of the richest spiritual and artistic storehouses of the Orthodox religion.

They contain historic heirlooms which have been lovingly cherished down the centuries. Those that have survived destruction and plunder bear living witness to the attainments of these monastic communities and in particular to the heights reached by religious art and aestheticism: ecclesiastical treasures, Gospel books with parchment pages illuminated with wonderful miniatures and initial letters, sacred vessels and gold chalices, crosses of carved wood and gold and silver and the caskets to contain them, silver Gospel book covers, epitaphioi embroidered in gold thread, liturgical vestments similarly embroidered all over, patriarchal chrysobulls, imperial sigilla, and delicately crafted censers.

Apart from the wall-paintings and portable ikons, the carved wooden ikonostases and ikon stands, and the episcopal thrones in churches, priceless works of art wrought with faith, patience, and piety form the material heritage of Greek Christianity on the Meteora.

There are in addition 1124 surviving codices — including, in the monastery of the Metamorphosis, the oldest dated Greek manuscript, written in 861 — which were studied and classified by the late academician Nikos Veis (1883-1958).

Not all the treasures of the Meteora can be listed in this limited space, but an indicative selection is given below.

Monastery of the Metamorphosis (Great Meteoron)

— Diptych ikon of the Virgin, the gift of Maria Palaiologina, sister of Ioasaph, founder of the monastery
— Fragment of a chrysobull bearing the signature of Emperor Andronikos Palaiologos
— Embroidered 14th-century epitaphios
— Large cross with scenes in silver and enamel (1595)
— Six leather-bound Gospels with gold tooling, printed in Venice (1745-1780)
— Portable ikons, including one of the Ascension of Christ "through the hand of" Vilistis (1772), Saint John the Theologian (1582), The Unfading Rose (1766), and four 16th-century ikons: The Nativity, The Crucifixion, Christ of Pity, and The Virgin Lamenting.

Monastery of Saint Stephen

— 17th-century illuminated manuscript
— Finely wrought censer
— Gold embroidered maniples and stoles
— Enamelled cross of 1765 with precious stones, decorated with religious scenes
— Cross with silver filigree work (1758)
— Three Gospels, one dated 1874, with various scenes
— Chalice (1631)
— Numerous portable ikons, including images of Jesus the Lifegiver, Saint George, Saint Charalambos, Saint Efthymios (1779) by the Blessed Alytios, Christ of Pity by Emmanouil Tzannes (1680), and the Virgin with the Divine Child (1680).

Monastery of Barlaam

— Epitaphios of green velvet with gold embroidery (1609)
— Ikons of Virgin with Angels by Emmanouil Tzannes (1668), Saints Dimitrios and Nestor, The Three Hierarchs, and others.

ΜΕΓΑΛΟ ΜΕΤΕΩΡΟ
600 ΧΡΟΝΙΑ

ΤΑ ΑΓΙΑ ΜΕΤΕΩΡΑ ΥΠΟΔΕΧΟΝΤ
ΤΟΥ ΓΕΝΟΥΣ

THE PATRIARCH OF THE ORTHODO
BY THE MONASTIC COMUNITIES C

AUF METEORA WIRD DER ÖKUM
EMPFANGEN

IL LUOGO SACRO DI METEORA F
AL PATRIARCA ECU

LE LIEU SACRÉ DES MÉTEORES D
AU PATRIARCHE DE L'

ΚΕΛΛΑΡΙ

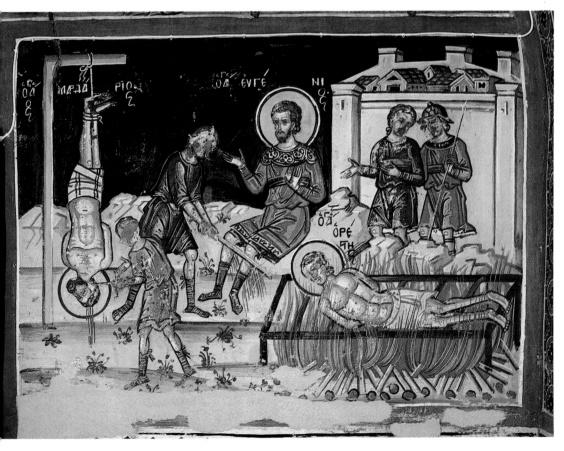

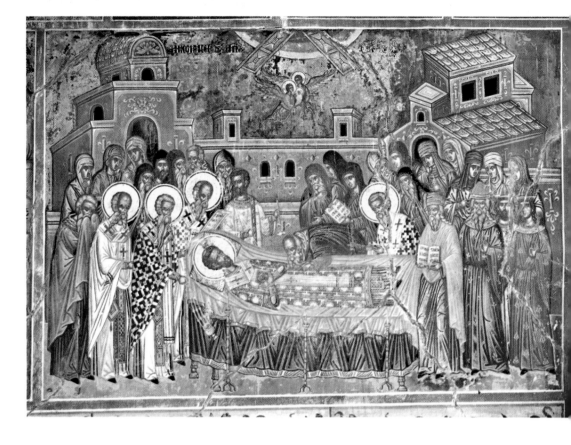

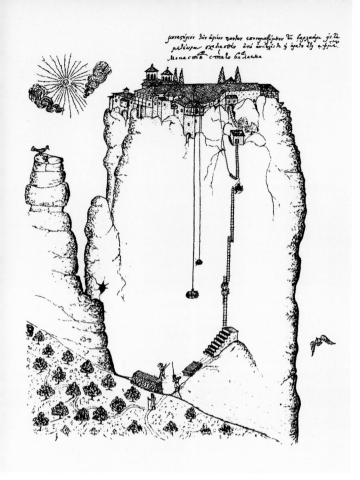

The monastery of Barlaam,
drawn by B. Barskij, 1745

THE HOLY MONASTERY OF
BARLAAM

In the mid 14th century the hermit Barlaam climbed the rock and built a few cells and a small chapel which he dedicated to the Three Hierarchs. He lived there in seclusion, dressed in tattered rags and lost in prayer till the end of his days.

The buildings remained deserted for many years after his death but early in the 16th century two brothers, the monks Nektarios and Theophanis, scions of the noble family of Apsarades from Ioannina who had already spent seven years on the column or rock of the Forerunner in the monastery of the Great Meteoron, ascended the rock and single-handed began to rebuild the church of the Three Hierarchs that Barlaam had erected.

The two brothers mention the ascent they made of the rock in their will:

"Having found the wide and lofty and tranquil rock, called Barlaam after the monk Barlaam who lived upon it long ago and from whom it received its name, to be of ample space and acceptable to us as a habitation though uninhabited for many years and utterly desolate as a building-ground, we commenced in 1518 to renovate and build upon it in order to make it habitable".

As time passed the monks increased in number till they were thirty in all, and then the two brothers built a second church, the katholikon, which is greater in width and has twin domes; they dedicated it in 1542 to All Saints.

The rapid growth of coenobitic life and the spiritual heights it attained there led to the monastery's enrichment by the two founders and by gifts from the faithful of estates, vineyards, olive groves, and metochia.

Even after their death — Theophanis died in 1544 and Nektarios in 1550 — the monastery continued to flourish, attracting yet more monks who obediently followed the instructions left by the founders in their will:

"...it is required that those who embrace the monastic life therein hold and perform all things in common, the fare at table, the clothing and footwear, the taking of decisions, the living quarters..."

J.J. Björnstaal visited Barlaam in 1779 and wrote a description of life in the monastery:

"The abbot of the monastery, Father Anatolios, who is also the sacristan and librarian, received me with every courtesy. There are two churches here. The monks are not above 9 or 10 in number and all the persons living up here on the rock do not exceed 24 individuals including the monastery servants. No woman has climbed up here since the founding of the monastery. Nor to the Meteoron. The abbot accompanied me to one of the churches which is not so large as that of the Meteoron but much more beautiful. It has two lovely small domes and is fairly well lit. Everywhere inside you see wall paintings in the local style, lacking perspective and shadowing. The Monastery of Barlaam was built 7044 years after the creation of the world, that is, in 1535 after Christ, as recorded in an inscription on a stone near the windlass with which they hoist you up...".

Immured in the sanctuary apse of the church of the Three Hierarchs, the first to be built on the rock, is a clay tile with the date 1627 on it, the year in which the building was restored. The church is a single-aisled basilica with a wooden ceiling and a wealth of finely executed wall-paintings.

Visitors are particularly struck by the unique artistry and beauty of two murals that adorn the interior of the church. The first is the Synaxis of Ephraim the Syrian, one of the most celebrated of ascetics and most prolific of authors among the Church Fathers, and the second the Dormition of Saint John Chrysostom.

In addition there are representations of many saints, of the founders Nektarios and Theophanis, of the Nativity of the Virgin and of Saint Nicholas of Metsovo who was martyred at Trikala.

In the account of their lives the founders Theophanis and Nektarios state that the church of All Saints built in 1542 was completed in twenty days.

It is of cruciform Athonite type with the dome over the main church resting on four columns and another dome over the narthex. There is a marvellous mural in the sanctuary

The tomb of the two founders Nektarios and Theophanis is in the south-east corner of the narthex. On the nearby wall are the ascetic figures of the two saints with snow-white beards holding the monastery between them.

The monastery of Barlaam

conch of the Virgin Platytera in a golden robe and just below it another of the Liturgy of the Angels. In the dome above the altar is an image of Jesus Christ also in robes of gold.

To the right and left of the main church are two semicircular choirs furnished with lecterns inlaid with ivory and mother-of-pearl.

The carved wooden ikonostasis is covered with gold paint; at the top of it is the Crucifixion scene, Christ's Mother and one of his beloved disciples standing beside the cross, while at the sides are full-figure images of Christ and the Mother of God interceding. In the four pendentives beneath the dome are the four Evangelists. The evangelist Luke is shown in a notable composition making the portrait of the Virgin.

There are other superb scenes apart from these, such as ones illustrating the life and sufferings of Christ, the Virgin of the Passion, and portraits of John of Damascus and Kosmas, both outstanding hymnists of the Church.

Above the Royal Doors leading into the sanctuary is a painting of the Dormition of the Virgin with clouds, shaped like animals and human beings, on which the Apostles are being borne to the bier on which her relics lie.

The narthex of the church is supported on four square columns. On the east wall is depicted the Second Coming; on the panel above the inner doorway is Saint Sisois in contemplation before the skeleton of Alexander the Great. In the south-west corner are scenes from the life of Saint John the Forerunner and in the north-west corner is the martyrdom of Saint Panteleimon. There is a picture on the left-hand column of the first founder Barlaam robed in pale coloured vestments.

The tomb of the two later founders Nektar-ios and Theophanis lies in the south-east corner of the narthex; on the nearby wall they are portrayed as ascetic figures with snow-white beards and holding the monastery in their hands.

Depicted in glowing colours upon their tomb is the expressive figure of a guardian angel, while a powerful Pantokrator looks down from the dome over the narthex.

Whoever the painter was who mentioned the founders' names in the inscription in the nave of the church did not add his own. Nonetheless, it is generally accepted that paintings in the sanctuary and the nave were done by Phrangos Katelanos, a leading exponent of the Cretan School, many of whose works are to be found in the monastery of the Great Lavra on Mount Athos. However, the paintings in the narthex were executed in 1566 by the priest Yiorgios, Sakellarios of Thebes, and his brother Phrangos (not to be confused with Katelanos).

The episcopal throne in the nave and the carved double doors of the narthex must not be overlooked.

Valuable objects such as carved wooden crosses, prelates' vestments, a bishop's throne inlaid with mother-of-pearl, an epitaphios of 1609 and portable ikons of the post-Byzantine period, the Gospel book once possessed by Emperor Constantine Porphyrogenitos, ecclesiastical vessels, and other such treasures are all displayed in the refectory.

This outstanding monastery was once noted for its attainments and exceptional organization, all of which it owed to its two founders Theophanis and Nektarios. In the course of time it became renowned as a model of a coenobitic institution.

The first rays of the sun light up the sky over the Meteora. The muffled beat of the semandron mingles with bird-song at dawn to announce another day of prayer and contemplation and spiritual exaltation.

The Day of Judgement

Christ in Glory

The rock crowned by the monastery of Barlaam

Christ the Overseer (1566)

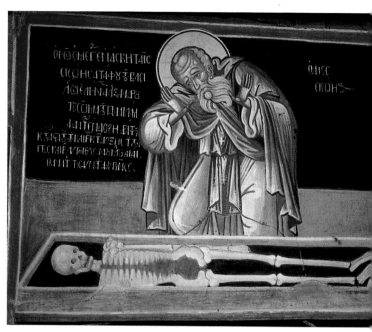

Blessed Sisois

Blessed Zosimas and Blessed Mary the Egyptian (1566)

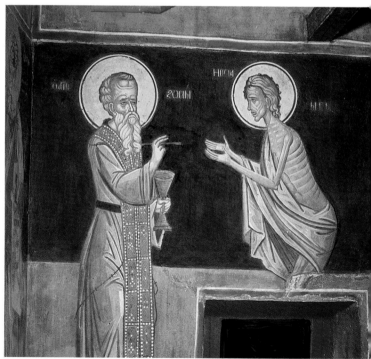

ΠΑΧΩΜΙΟΣ

The martyrdom of saints

*Saint Pachomios
and the Angel
of the Lord*

69

An aspect of monastic life..

Study and contemplation

The katholikon
of Barlaam

The outsize 16th-century
barrel in the monastery cel-
lar with a capacity of 13,000
litres

ΟΥ ΧΥ ΧΑΛΚΩ ΧΑΡΑΧΘΕΙΣΑ ΕΝ ΠΛΥΗ ΙΕΡΑ ΜΟΝΗ ΣΥΜΠΕΡΕΧΟΥΣΑ ΕΠΙ ΚΑΤΑ ΠΛΗΣΙΟΝ ΕΥΡΙΣΚΟΜΕΝΑ ΕΤΕΡΑ ΙΕΡΑ ΜΟΝΑΣΤΗΡΑ ΤΗΣ Ε ΠΑΡ
ΝΑΧΟΙΣ ΚΑΙ ΣΚΕΘΟ ΦΥΛΑΚΟΣ ΠΣ ΑΥΤΗΣ ΜΟΝΗΣ ΚΥΡ ΔΑΝΙΗΛ, ΚΑΙ ΔΑΠΑΝΗΣ ΤΟΥ ΤΗ ΜΙΩ ΤΑ ΤΟΥ Κ ΧΡΕΣΙΜΩ ΤΑ ΤΟΥ ΚΥΡ ΦΙΛΟΥ
ΠΤΑΚΟΣΙΟΣ Ω ΟΓΔΟΗΚΟΣΩ ΔΕΥΤΕΡΩ ΚΑΤΑ ΜΗΝΑ ΙΟΥΝΙΟΝ 21

+ μοναστήριον

*The monastery of the Metamorphos[is]
a 1745 sketch by B. Barskij*

THE HOLY MONASTERY OF
THE METAMORPHOSIS
(THE GREAT METEORON)

The summit of the sheer rock on which the monastery of the Metamorphosis of the Saviour, known as the Great Meteoron, has been built is about 60 stremmata (6 hectares) in extent. It lies 613 metres above sea-level and 400 above the centre of Kalambaka town.

The rock used to be called Platys Litho[s] (literally, Broad Stone), but Athanasios, late[r] Saint Athanasios the Meteorite, who first se[t]tled upon it renamed it Meteoron (meteor o[r], as here, mid-air) because it was higher tha[n] all the others around it.

View from the north-east of the Monastery of the Metamorphosis

In former times the ascent was by hanging ladders or a net (called the vrizoni) in which visitors, baggages, and supplies were hoisted up to the monastery with the help of a windlass. However, since 1923 a short tunnel and 146 steps cut into the rock have made the ascent somewhat easier.

The katholikon of the monastery, the church of the Metamorphosis, first built by Athanasios, was later rebuilt from the very foundations, as we learn from an inscription on the south wall of the sanctuary:

"THIS NEW AND MUCH VENERATED CHURCH OF OUR LORD JESUS CHRIST WAS ERECTED FROM ITS FOUNDATIONS THROUGH THE TOIL AND AT THE EXPENSE OF THE MOST BLESSED OF OUR FATHERS AND FOUNDERS ATHANASIOS AND IOASAPH IN THE YEAR 1388 AND WAS REBUILT AND REDECORATED THROUGH THE SOLICITUDE AND AT THE PAINS OF THE LEAST OF BROTHERS IN 1484 SECOND INDICTION THE 20TH DAY OF THE MONTH OF NOVEMBER."

The church is built in the Athonite style, cruciform with a twelve-sided dome and conchs at the sides.

The narthex is supported by four columns, all its walls and ceiling being decorated with religious scenes and the martyrdoms of saints.

In the left-hand conch is Saint John the Forerunner and over the central doorway Christ with the Forerunner and the Virgin. In the right-hand conch is the Baptism of Christ with the Jordan River personified, while Archangel Gabriel is portrayed over the right-hand door and Archangel Michael over the left-hand.

To the left and right of the central doorway is a magnificent representation of the Annunciation of the Virgin joyfully receiving the salutation of Archangel Gabriel.

The monastery of the Metamorphosis

On the north side of the narthex is the tomb of the monastery's founders, Athanasios and Ioasaph. Next to it is a wall-painting portraying their ascetic figures: Athanasios on the left, Ioasaph on the right, holding between them a replica of the monastery. There are also many-figured compositions relating the lives of various saints.

The sanctuary, which is 10 metres wide, is adorned with murals of the highest quality. Military saints wearing Serbian belts and headgear, possibly because Ioasaph was of Serbian origin, are depicted in the conch. There are depictions also of the Three Hierarchs and above them of the Eucharist and the Ascension, and higher still the Virgin Platytera.

On the west wall are portrayed the founders of the monastery, "Athanasios our Blessed father and Master of the Holy Meteoron" and "Ioasaph our Blessed father", as they are characteristically inscribed. Opposite them on the two columns are Saint Nicholas "The Ardent Protector" and the Virgin Paraclete (Suppliant).

The main church is of the inscribed cross type with dome and lateral conchs and is filled with splendid wall-paintings (1552) executed by an unknown artist. Excluding the sanctuary, it is 32 metres long. The twelve-sided dome is supported on four columns and rises to a height of 24 metres.

The imposing Pantokrator in the dome is surrounded by angelic powers. In the right-hand choir are portrayed the Resurrection of Lazarus, the Entry into Jerusalem and the Last Supper, while in the left are the Descent of Christ into Hades and scenes of his appearance after the Resurrection.

The bishop's throne of carved wood is an exceptionally fine work of art, very grand in conception and inlaid with mother-of-pearl. It is inscribed with the phrase IC XC NIKA (Jesus Christ Conquers) and the year 1616.

Of equal merit as a work of art is the carved and gilded wooden ikonostasis erected in 1791 and decorated with animal figures and plant motifs.

The hermitage of Saint Athanasios, a small half-ruined building set back into the rock, is at the entrance to the monastery. The cavern was once the saint's hermitage; behind the entrance are a tiny chapel and the ossuary.

Other monastic buildings include the small chapel of the Forerunner, built against the south wall of the katholikon and containing a mural of the Pantokrator with angels stood around an Old Testament, and a carved wooden ikonostasis, and to the west of the katholikon the single-aisled chapel of Saints Constantine and Helen with a polygonal exterior dome and, again, a carved wooden screen.

The kitchen, one of the oldest of the monastic buildings, is a small vaulted space. The centre is occupied by a great hearth; on it there used to stand the large cauldron in which the monks prepared their frugal meals. Adjacent to the kitchen is the refectory, thirty metres long and twelve wide; it terminates in a conch in which are depicted the archangels Michael and Gabriel.

The monolithic table at which the abbot sat down to eat and the two long narrow ones at which the monks sat still exist.

The monastic infirmary behind the refectory was contructed in 1572. The whole of the lower floor is in existence today while only sections of the upper one remain. Four columns in the main chamber, on the lower floor, support eight small domes with tile decoration. There used to be a little chapel on the first floor dedicated to the Aghioi Anargyroi (Saints Kosmas and Damianos). The old refectory has now been converted into a museum where the monastery's treasures are preserved.

Over the monastery cellars, once full of wine barrels, are the monks' old cells with a low door and small window in each. The tower containing the windlass still stands, as does the bakehouse which used to produce hundreds of loaves of bread every day for both the community and its guests.

The Last Supper

The archangel Michael

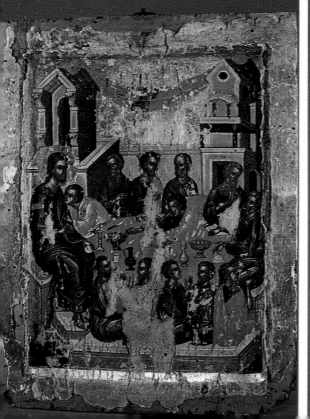

View of the monastery of the Metamorphosis

Transfiguration of the Saviour

The Three Hierarchs

Ascent by net

The earliest ascetics ascended the rocks by means of successive tiers of scaffolding supported on timbers wedged into crevices. Traces of such scaffolding can still be seen today.

Later they replaced the scaffolding with immensely long hanging ladders which induced fits of vertigo in some climbers. Those not bold enough to ascend by way of the hanging ladders were hauled up in a net, a process that lasted about half an hour, a half hour of anxiety and fear. The passenger might break out in a cold sweat when the net spun in the void as it left the ground, while the rope coiled around the windlass taughtened and shrilled, threatening at any moment to cast him into the abyss.

However, in 1922 steps were cut out of the rock face, so nowadays the visitor climbs up with ease and in safety, the net still being used for the carriage of food and other necessities of the monastery.

The Holy Monasteries of
Barlaam and the Metamorphosis
viewed from the air

The Nativity

A sense of peace and a pricking of the conscience overwhelm the visitor as the feeble flames of multi-coloured lampions flicker in the unearthly gloom casting their light on the ascetic figures of saints. The golden ikonostases and ikon-stands, the halos and the ex-votos of the faithful glimmer in the dimness, while the exquisite fragrance of incense wafts about the reverent worshipper.

The interior of the Katholikon, Monastery of the Metamorphosis

Carved wooden cross

Deisis

The Virgin Lamenting (14th-c. portable ikon)

Christ of Pity (14th-c. portable ikon)

The martyrdom of saints

View of the monastery

THE HOLY MONASTERY OF
THE VIRGIN YPAPANTI

The monastery lies half an hour distant from the monastery of the Metamorphosis and is seldom visited by pilgrims as it is now virtually closed to the public.

All the monastery buildings lie crowded together within a large and narrow but deep cave in the side of a massive sheer rock. Behind the entrance are the ruins of the refectory, the bake-house, and two rows of cells; the katholikon and, on the south side, more cells lie beyond a narrowing of the cave.

The monastery was founded in the 14th century by the hieromonk Neilos and the abbot of the monastery of the Theotokos Doupiani. The whole of the interior is covered by well-preserved wall-paintings of an exceptionally decorative character.

On the same rock to the east lie the ruins of the monastery of Saint Dimitrios destroyed by the infamous Ali Pasha of Ioannina because the rebel chieftain Papa-Efthymios Vlachavas had set up his headquarters there during Greece's struggle for independence from the Turks (1821-1827).

The Descent into Hades

Wall-paintings in the katholikon

Entry into Jerusalem

The monastery of Rousanou

The Meteora landscape, consisting of sharply contrasting geological features, is a scene of unparalleled beauty and grandeur.

The scenery suggests a vision of the world in the first days of the Creation and puts one in mind of the lost state of human innocence and perfection, of the decay of the human condition.

As we look upon this sacred site our hearts are overwhelmed with a sense of childlike simplicity and genuine wonderment. Detached from the miracles wrought by faith, our thoughts turn to the infinite and the eternal and our soul communes with the silence. The scene rises sheer before us, drawing us into direct contact with the Creator.

On these heights, where nature may express itself in sudden violence or in utter stillness, individuals who have turned their backs upon the world have lived since early times and have passed into eternity by way of self-denial, seclusion, and prayer. Their total dedication to God moved divinely inspired hands to create unsurpassed masterpieces of art: wall-paintings, portable ikons, and wood carvings adorn the monastic churches while gold, silver, and marble — gifts of the faithful — have been transformed with skill and patience into votive offerings expressing the gratitude of humble monks and pilgrims of the Orthodox faith.

The monastery of Aghia Triada

The monastery of Aghia Triada,
a sketch by B. Barskij, 1745

THE HOLY MONASTERY OF

AGHIA TRIADA
(THE HOLY TRINITY)

The rock on which the monastery of Aghia Triada stands presents the most attractive and characteristic picture of the Meteora.

The landscape is incomparably beautiful and picturesque. In the foreground is the breathtaking rock surmounted by Aghia Triada, in the background the valley of the Pineios river overlooked by the soaring peaks of the Pindos mountain range and its thickly wooded slopes.

From the rock itself the view is unrivalled. Fear mingled with pure delight seizes you as you gaze down from the edge of the rock into the Thessalian plain stretching away hazily southwards. The entire length of the Agrapha mountains reaches out to the peak of Mount Koziaka opposite; you feel as if you are suspended in space as you look down on the houses of Kalambaka four hundred metres directly beneath you.

The small church of Saint John the Forerunner (Prodromos) is the first building one meets on entering the monastery. According to the inscription on the inner wall above the entrance, first recorded by the French 19th-century archaeologist L. Heuzey when he visited the place in 1864, this tiny church was quarried from the rock itself and its walls were decorated in 1682. Heuzey reproduced the inscription in his book "Les Météores":

"+ THROUGH THE HAND OF NIKODIMOS A POOR AND RAGGED MONK 1682."

Before the church was carved out of the rock this space was very probably a hermit's dwelling.

We know nothing for certain regarding the foundation of the monastery, but historical sources point to it having been built between the years 1458 and 1476. We have no evidence for the tradition that the founder was a monk called Dometios.

The top of the rock is five or six stremmata in extent and on it are situated the two churches of the monastery, the refectory, the tower with the windlass, cells, water cisterns, and ancillary buildings.

In earlier times pilgrims ascended by ladder or net, but in 1925 under abbot Nikandor the monks carved out of the rock one hundred and forty steps which led up to the monastery from a narrow footpath at its base.

The katholikon, dedicated to the name of the Holy Trinity (Aghia Triada), stands in the north-western corner. It is a small church built in the Byzantine style being cruciform with twin columns and a low dome; it consists of a nave, narthex, and sacristy.

There is a gilded ikonostasis in the tiny nave hung with an ikon of Christ to the right of the Royal Doors (1662) and with another of the Virgin (1718), painted "through the hand of Rizos the least of mortals from the province of Agrapha" according to the inscription on the back of the ikon. Other noteworthy ikons on the screen are those of the Aghia Triada and of Christ dressed in the local karagouni costume.

An old Gospel book with a silver cover, printed in Venice in 1539, rests on the ikon-stand. There are depictions of the Pantokrator and of the four Evangelists in the dome, with Luke shown painting the Virgin. There is an expressionistic representation of the Behead-ing of the Forerunner hanging by the right-hand lectern.

According to another inscription in the church, the wall-paintings were done in 1741 by the priest Antonios and his brother Nicholas. There is an inscription on the inner wall over the doorway of the narthex with its barrel-vaulted roof which records that the narthex was built in 1689 and embellished with wall-paintings in 1692. In accordance with the inscription on the west wall the sacristy to the right of the sanctu-ary was built in 1684. But the priceless objects it once contained — such as precious crosses, sac-red vestments, old codices and manuscripts, candlestands, chalices, and other objects of great intrinsic and artistic value — were pillaged in the course of foreign occupation in the 1940s and by other unknown sacrilegious persons who made off with even the monastery bell. However, 26 old ikons now in Barlaam monastery and forty manuscripts that have been transferred to Saint Stephen's were saved. The skull of Saint Tryphon also escaped the pillage.

The ascent to the monastery

The monastery of Saint Stephen, a sketch by B. Barskij, 1745

THE HOLY MONASTERY OF

SAINT STEPHEN

The monastery of Saint Stephen, the richest on the Meteora, stands on an immense rock overlooking Kalambaka.

Situated on the south side of the Meteora, it is the most accessible of all the monasteries to the visitor, who is able to reach the entrance without any difficulty. Saint Stephen's is also linked by a permanent bridge, eight metres in length, to Koukoula Hill opposite.

Until 1927 there was an inscribed tablet set into the stone arch over the ancient outer iron gateway which read: 6770 IEREMIAS. This inscription informs us that in the year 6770 since the creation of the world, otherwise in 1192 A.D., the hermit Ieremias was living there, and that in that year the first settlers upon the rock, with Ieremias at their head, established the hermitage, erecting a few cells, a cistern in which to collect water, and the small chapel of Saint Stephen.

The foundation of the monastery itself is dated to some time in the 14th century. It was built by Antonios Katakouzinos and Philotheos of Siatena who are portrayed in the small church.

Antonios Katakouzinos was the son of the Serbian ruler Nikiphoros I and nephew of Symeon Uroš, father of Ioasaph, one of the founders of the monastery of the Great Meteoron. He was of Byzantine descent through his mother Maria, daughter of the emperor John Katakouzinos VI who is mentioned in a manuscript liturgy belonging to the monastery in which it is recorded that it was written in the year 1404 "by Antonios Katakouzinos founder of Saint Stephen's". This manuscript is now one of the treasures of the monastery.

The second-named founder, Philotheos, is referred to in a letter written by Ieremias I, patriarch of Constantinople, as restorer of Saint Stephen's "from the very foundations".

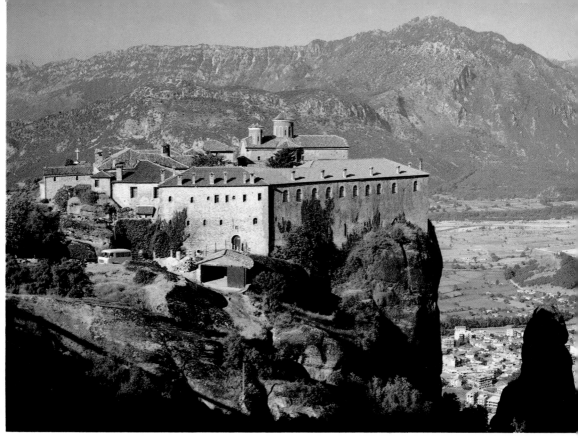

View of the monastery

Zosimas, who came from Mount Pelion and was a monk of Esphigmenou monastery on Mount Athos, relates that the Byzantine emperor Andronikos Palaiologos (1328-1341) visited the monastery in 1333 when he came to Thessaly. Moved by the warmth of the hospitality he received from the monks and their abbot, he presented several estates and large sums of money to the monastery which ever since has been titled "imperial". Later, in 1545, the patriarch Ieremias pronounced the monastery "stavropegic" — that is, "patriarchal" and thus independent of the diocesan bishop of Stagi.

The church of Saint Charalambos was erected in 1798, since when the monastery has been known as the monastery of Saint Stephen and Saint Charalambos.

In 1850 the monastery built at its own expense the Konstantion School in Kalambaka, donating at the same time 80,000 gold drachmae for the founding of a Gymnasion (secondary school) in Trikala.

While there were thirty-one monks residing in the monastery around 1880, by 1960 it was almost deserted. This led to it being converted in the following year into a convent, today a flourishing community.

The small chapel of Saint Stephen, erected in the 15th century, in the eastern quarter, was built as a basilica with a single aisle and a wooden ceiling. A triple arched doorway joins the narthex and the nave which is entirely covered with fine wall-paintings, some of which have survived in good condition though many, especially on the south side, have from time to time suffered wear and tear at the hands of impious raiders or have been overpainted.

There are some magnificent murals in a fair state of preservation depicting the full-length figures of saints, the Akathistos Hymn, and the Virgin Platytera. On the left of the narthex door there are portrayals of the archangel Gabriel and next to him of the monastery's second founder Antonios Katakouzinos, while to the right are the archangel Michael and the first founder Philotheos.

The wooden ikonostasis in the church, carved with plant and animal motifs, was erected in the 17th century; it is surmounted by a cross. The screen is hung with three rows of small ikons depicting the prophets, the apostles, and the Dodekaorton (Twelve Great Feasts of the Church).

The bishop's throne and the lecterns are inlaid with mother-of-pearl; the upper part of the throne is inscribed:

"THIS THRONE OF THE FIRST MARTYR SAINT STEPHEN WAS MADE WITH THE ASSISTANCE AND AT THE EXPENSE OF..."

The rest of the inscription is missing.

The church of Saint Charalambos, the katholikon of the monastery, is an inscribed cross with a central dome and two smaller ones. Built in 1798, it is fairly spacious, its length being 20 metres, and is the most recent such church among the monasteries of the Meteora.

There are so few murals that the church can hardly be considered as embellished with religious paintings. The Pantokrator and the four Evangelists are depicted in the central dome.

An exceptionally well-carved wooden ciborium overhangs the sanctuary altar on which there rests the skull of Saint Stephen.

The ikon screen which separates the sanctuary from the body of the church is of carved wood and terminates at the top in a gilded crucifix. It is ornamented with stylized plant and animal motifs and symbols of the Last Supper and hung with ikons of Saint Dimitrios, Stephen the first martyr, and other saints.

There is an inscription carved on a wooden panel above the ikon of Saint Charalambos which reads:

"THE IKONOSTASIS OF THE CHURCH OF SAINT CHARALAMBOS WAS MADE AT THE EXPENSE OF KYRIOS GAVRIEL BISHOP OF STAGI DURING THE ABBACY OF KYRIOS THEOPHANIS HIEROMONK FROM THE REGION OF SOULATENA, TRIKKI, BY THE HANDS OF MASTROKOSTAS AND DIMITRIS FROM THE VILLAGE OF METSOVON IN THE YEAR 1814."

Some damaged ikons belonging to the ikonostasis have been replaced by ikons painted in recent years by Greek religious artists, such as those of Christ and the Theotokos, both executed by K. Xynopoulos (1960), and of the Forerunner and Saint Charalambos (1965), by I. Karoussos.

The carved wooden episcopal throne and the cantors' lecterns are inlaid with mother-of-pearl. The four ikon-stands, also of carved wood, were made in 1836. Two of them, in the choirs to the left and right, are inlaid with ivory and mother-of-pearl. Carved into the floor of the church is a roundel featuring the double-headed eagle signifying that the monastery enjoyed the patronage of Byzantine emperors.

Four columns support the plain ceiling of the narthex. Three doorways lead into the body of the church where there are two carved wooden stands on which rest ikons of Christ and the Virgin.

In recent years the monastic refectory has housed a display of valuable objects and treasures including post-Byzantine ikons, rare manuscripts, liturgical vestments, carved wooden crosses, and other such items.

Among other buildings are the calefactory and on the south side the fairly spacious guest quarters which include the visitors' reception room and the bishop's lodgings, a small room in which the Metropolitan stays whenever he visits the monastery.

Mention must be made here of the important religious and social work performed nowadays by the convent of Saint Stephen, work which includes the cultivation of and instruction in Byzantine music and hagiography and even the writing of religious books by well-educated nuns, among whom are both professors and doctors.

View of the monastery

Saint Charalambos with scenes of his martyrdom

The Royal Doors leading into the sanctuary

Jesus Christ the Lifegiver

Christ of Pity

MONASTERY OF THE PANTOKRATOR

Delapidated walls are all that remain of the monastery of the Pantokrator on the north side of the rock of Doupiani. A tattered will in the monastery of the Metamorphosis confirms that the founder was the hieromonk Neophytos. There is mention also of the monk Serapion in a contemporary history of 1436. The 1650 Register of the Meteora place it first in the list of monasteries.

AGHIA MONI (Holy Monastery)

This monastery, of which there are few remains today, once crowned a vertical rock below the monasteries of Barlaam and Metamorphosis. A sigillum of the Oecumenical Patriarch Timotheos dated 1614 records that more than twenty hieromonks and monks rebuilt it from the foundations and dedicated it to the name of the Virgin.

MONASTERY OF THE VIRGIN YPSILOTERA KALLIGRAPHON

This monastery possessed a scriptorum, a workshop devoted to the practice of calligraphy and the copying of manuscripts, which produced some fine codices that have survived into our own day. The founder was one Paschalis of Kalambaka who built the monastery in 1347. On the giant rock that rears up to the southeast of the monastery of Metamorphosis there are today only ruins.

MONASTERY OF SAINT MODESTOS

The monastery of Saint Modestos on top of the tall rock opposite the monastery of Aghia Triada now lies in ruins. In a 12th-century letter it is referred to as "the land of Saint Modestos". It is listed in 1614 in a sigillum of Patriarch Timotheos II and in the Register of that same year.

MONASTERY OF THE FORERUNNER

The small monastery of the Forerunner once stood on a large rock beside the monastery of Saint Nicholas Anapafsas; its ruins may still be seen. Various codices and a report addressed to Ioannis Vassileios, voivode of Moldo-Wallachia, confirm it was built between 1634 and 1653.

MONASTERY OF PALAIOPANAGHIA

The small rock-carved church with its dome and wall-paintings is situated in the locality of Mykani between the villages of Vlachava and Asprokklisia in the region of Chasia. In a decree issued by the Serbian Uroš Dušan in 1358 and in another issued by his brother Symeon in 1362 there is a reference to the "Cave known as Kyrillou, in the locality of Mykaina". The church is mentioned also by Neophytos, bishop of Larisa, in a manuscript dated 1541, and again in the 1650 Register preserved at the monastery of the Metamorphosis.

MONASTERY OF SAINT NICHOLAS BANDOVA-KOPHINA

In a cave on a rock lying between Kalambaka and Kastraki is the ruined church of Saint Nicholas of Bandova. The approach to it passes through three caves linked by wooden ladders, the last of which leads up to the platform of the monastery, site of the old windlass which used to haul up the monks in a net, and to a cistern for rain water.

The monastery must have been founded in about 1400 A.D. It is listed in a 17th-century register now in the monastery of the Metamorphosis (Inv. no. 372). The occupying forces bombarded the monastery in 1943 causing irreparable damage. The tiny church is quarried out of the solid rock. An inscription over the doorway reads:

THIS MONASTERY OF SAINT NICHOLAS BANDOVA WAS RESTORED WITH THE AS-SISTANCE OF THE MONK IGNATIOS WHO ONCE SERVED IN THE MONASTERY OF SAINT STEPHEN AND LATER CAME HERE 1876."

MONASTERY OF SAINT GRIGORIOS AND SAINT ANTONY

Remains of wooden balconies and hanging ladders in caves on another immensely tall rock bear witness to the former monastery of Saint Grigorios, while east of it in the same rock complex there was once the monastery of Saint Antony of which only the small church survives today in a fair state of preservation. According to tradition these monasteries were built in the 14th century.

MONASTERY OF THE HOLY APOSTLES

Looking up from Kalambaka one can make out the quarried stairway, cisterns, and remnants of wall-paintings on the giant rock known as Aghia. Neophytos, bishop of Larisa, mentions the monastery in a letter of his dated 1551. It is also listed in the Register of 1650 kept at the monastery of the Metamorphosis, appearing as "The Holy Apostles' called Kallistou", the name by which it was referred to a century earlier, in 1547, on the cover of an evangelium.

MONASTERY OF SAINT PETER ON ALYSOS

The vast outcrop of rock known as Alysos which looks down upon Kalambaka was once crowned by the monastery of the Adoration of Saint Peter. It was built about 1400 and lies 13th in the list of monasteries occurring in the Register of 1650.

MONASTERY OF THE HOLY SPIRIT

The ascent to the small church which is still standing is a very difficult one as the rock it is on is more than 300 metres high. A dangerous narrow pathway quarried from the rock leads the visitor to this remote spot. The wall-paintings are entirely destroyed. Every feature of the church has been carved from the natural rock: the altar, the ikon-stand, two rain water cisterns, and the tomb in which the founder lies. There are some ruined cells to be seen and a large iron cross which tradition holds was set up by Stefan Dušan, "Emperor of the Serbs and Greeks".

GLOSSARY

Aghía Triáda	Holy Trinity
´Aghioi Anárgyroi	"Holy Moneyless Ones": saints unpaid for their services
Akáthistos Hymn	hymn to Virgin sung standing ('Not seated')
anchorite	hermit, ascetic
Anapafsás	from 'anápafsis' = rest, peace
Athonite	pertaining to Mount Athos (see below)
basilica	early Christian church following architectural form of an ancient temple
calefactory	room warmed by open fire
calligraphy	fine script, as practised by medieval copyists
censer	incense burner, thurible
chrysobull	'golden seal': document with imperial or ecclesiastical seal
ciborium	canopy over altar or throne
codex	manuscript volume (usually of ancient texts)
coenobium	community performing and owning all things in common
conch	semicircular apse with half-dome at top
Déisis	Supplication, Intercession
despot	once autocratic ruler, now diocesan bishop
diptych	two-leaved (ikon), folding like a book
Dodekáorton	Twelve Great Feasts of the Church
Dormition (of Virgin)	'Falling asleep': Assumption into Heaven
epitáphios	pall, embroidered cloth portraying bier of Christ
evangelium	book of Gospels
hagiography	art of writing or illustrating saints' lives
hierarch	archangel or prelate (esp. Fathers of the Church)
ikón	painted image of saint or sacred figure
ikonóstasis	screen on which ikons are hung
karagoúni	'black cape' of Thessalian plainsfolk
katholikón	main church of monastery
labarum	processional banner
maniple	liturgical vestment hanging over left arm
Metéora	here 'suspended in mid-air'
Meteorite	member of Meteora monastic community
metóchi	dependency of a monastery
metropolitan	bishop of a province
Mount Athos	exclusively monastic community in N. Greece
narthex	ante-chamber at west end of church
pendentive	architectural feature supporting dome
Platytéra	'Wider than the Heavens' (attribute of Virgin)
Pródromos	The Forerunner (St John the Baptist)
Protáton	main church (as in Karyes, Mount Athos)
Prótos	superior of a monastic community
Royal Doors	double doors in ikonostasis (between nave and sanctuary)
Sakellários	an office held by Church elder
sémandron	wooden gong
sigillum	seal, signet
skete	hermitage with chapel and supporting land
stavropegic	of a monastery directly subordinate to Patriarchate of Constantinople
stole	long liturgical vestment suspended from neck
strémma	land measure: one-tenth of hectare
sýnaxis	gathering, choir of angels
Theotókos	Mother of God
voivode	local governor, ruler of Moldo-Wallachia in Ottoman times
Ypapantí	Presentation of the Virgin

TRANSLATOR'S NOTE

The transliteration of Greek proper names poses many problems and leads to several inconsistencies. Every writer evolves his own conventions, sometimes at variance with one another.

The accentation of Greek words directly transliterated into English is shown only in the Glossary.

Here the single s in words such as Larisa, Athanasios, and Rousanou is pronounced as is the double ss in Thessaly, that is, as a soft sound.

I have ignored the fact that the town of Trikala (as it appears throughout the text) sometimes occurs in Greek as Trikkala; and one or two other such simplifications have been made.

The "Date of the Creation" indicated in a number of inscriptions is not always the same. This may reflect a miscalculation on the part of the author of the inscribed text or a misreading (or misinterpretation) of the Byzantine alphabetic numerals when they were copied out.